Y0-ABL-854

look at us, Lord

robert marshall haven

photographs by james r. finney
design by nancy r. bozeman

abingdon press

nashville and new york

look at us, Lord

Copyright © 1969 by Abingdon Press

All rights in this book are reserved.
No part of the book may be
reproduced in any manner whatsoever without
written permission of the publishers
except brief quotations
embodied in critical articles or reviews.
For information address Abingdon
Press, Nashville, Tennessee.

Standard Book Number: 687-22616-3

Library of Congress Catalog Card Number: 69-19736

Set up, printed, and bound by the
Parthenon Press, at Nashville, Tennessee
United States of America

for Sallie, beloved wife and companion

foreword

There are in life certain crises or climactic experiences
which come to every man and which begin with
birth and proceed through adolescence and the
educational years to adulthood, culminating with old
age and death. Usually the parish clergyman is
with his people in these experiences at each stage in life.
He is there at the beginning and he is there at the end.
It is up to him to minister to his people as they
move into and through the high and low points in their lives,
and this is both the joy and burden of the parish
ministry. The parish church when it functions properly is
irrevocably tied to these experiences, and any man
who has ever served as a parish clergyman knows
the deep sense of meaning which comes from being with
his people at these times. That is why I believe in the
parish. The parish clergy through the liturgy and the pastoral
ministry of the Church are where the action is
in the lives of their people.

But of course in these human crisis situations there are
frequently deep questions that arise which
the clergyman must face as he stands by his people and which
often leave him with a sense of frustration, failure,
and inadequacy. How does one explain, for example,
premature death or loneliness or job lay-offs?

How does one explain the inability of the Church to respond
to a person in need? By the very nature of his vocation
the parish clergyman must continuously
face questions of this sort to which there are
no easy answers and to which,
he sometimes feels, there might not be any answers whatever.
So he cries out in his frustration
and in his sense of inadequacy, and leaves the parish
for less demanding fields.

I have known these dark moments. My life as an Episcopal
student and priest through five parishes is steeped
in them. I too have cried out.
I too as a parish clergyman have faced with my people
the inequities of life, the sufferings of the innocent,
and the countless failures of God's Church.
I too have sometimes thought seriously
of abandoning the parish church.

I hope I do not sound pietistic when I say
that prayer has been an answer for me and that prayer has
become in my ministry an inestimable source of strength.
I do not think that prayer has necessarily given
any packaged solutions, but it has given
a sense of strength and renewal. The poem-prayers

of this book were initially a catharsis for me as I poured out
on paper and before the depths of the Lord
my own experiences in the parish church
grappling with the failures of the Church and with the deep
human problems to which the parish priest
is called to minister. In the writing of these prayers
there came for me renewal and insight and a deeper grasp
of the meaning of the Lord for our age and the proper place
of the parish church in our society.
In the writing of these prayers there came for me a sense of
the beauty of the Lord I had never known before.
This beauty can immeasurably strengthen the life of any man.
That is why I believe in prayer.

Is all this too simple? Perhaps.
I am not a theologian. Nonetheless, this is the frame of
reference and life style and the thinking through
which these poem-prayers have been created. They represent the
world of a typical parish minister, and they describe
situations within the parish ministry from childhood across
the life span of man to death. The book is a Lord view
of life and is consequently a book of joy and pain,
faith and doubt, success and failure, laughter and tears.

robert marshall haven
amsterdam, new york

This child, Lord,
has come to the
altar rail with
his mother, his
hand in hers.
I have never seen
him here before.
He is so young.
His eyes peer
quickly about
with anticipation
and with awe.
I place my hand upon
his head as he kneels
before me, asking
that you, Lord,
will bless him
and keep him.
He looks up at me
and as he does
he smiles.
In that smile, Lord,
I can see my
ministry.
In that smile, Lord,
your vast
mysteries
suddenly lie
bare and simple
and sure.

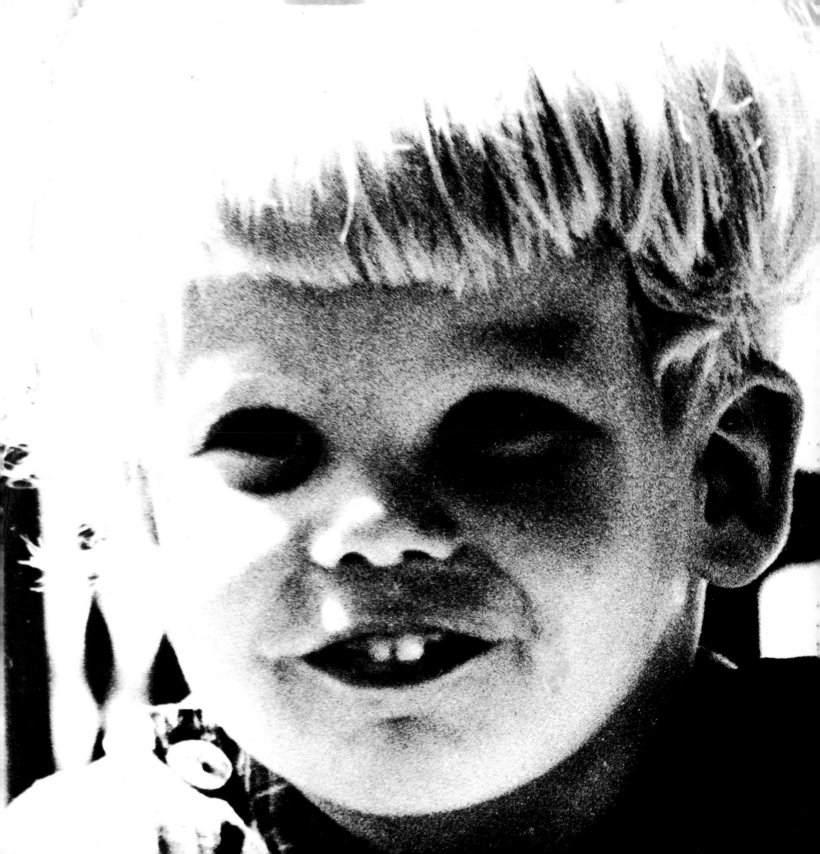

This baby, Lord, is
a thalidomide baby.
Perfectly well and
formed. The mother is
a German married to a
soldier. She had the
courage to go through
with it all when it
would have been easier
to have done otherwise.
She stands here with
her baby before the
font. The little baby
sleeps in his blanket
as he is born again by
water and is made an
inheritor of your
kingdom.

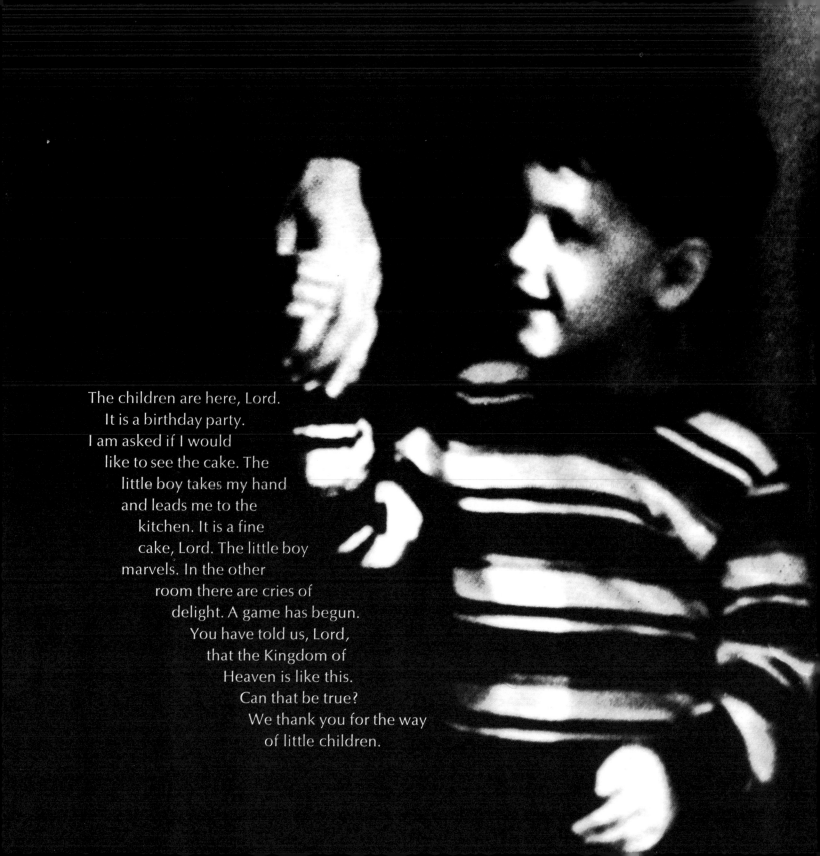

The children are here, Lord.
It is a birthday party.
I am asked if I would
like to see the cake. The
little boy takes my hand
and leads me to the
kitchen. It is a fine
cake, Lord. The little boy
marvels. In the other
room there are cries of
delight. A game has begun.
You have told us, Lord,
that the Kingdom of
Heaven is like this.
Can that be true?
We thank you for the way
of little children.

This boy has cerebral palsy, Lord.
He is four years old.
He is sitting in his wheelchair with a
strap across his chest.
I watch his grotesque writhings and his
spasms which jerk him about abruptly
like a multijointed puppet
on strings.
His mother tells him to sit up.
In her voice, Lord, there is
a note
of impatience.

He has hemophilia, Lord.
He's only six years old.
There are needles in his legs.
On his frail body one can
see angry bruises.
He asks if he can read to me.
As he reads slowly through
his first grade book
there is about him
something valiant.
He smiles with delight as
I praise him.
He has been here for
three weeks. Transfusion
upon transfusion. His
bleeding is uncontrolled.
He's only a little boy, Lord,
with his first grade book
awaiting death.

It is the Christmas party, Lord.
Ice cream, games, and Christmas tree.
The little colored girl is
laughing, Lord.
She has never played musical
chairs before. Excitement
emanates from her as she rushes
about in time to the music of
the parish piano. Successfully
she finds a chair and laughs
again.
For this small child, Lord,
musical chairs are an outward
and visible sign of you.

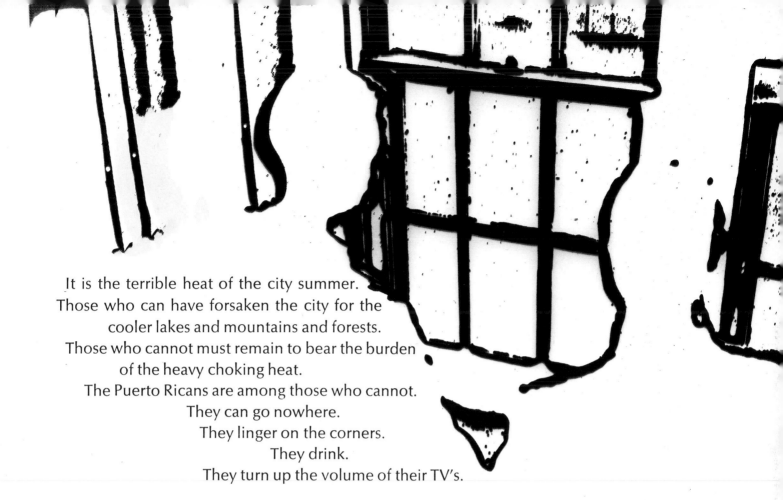

It is the terrible heat of the city summer.
Those who can have forsaken the city for the
cooler lakes and mountains and forests.
Those who cannot must remain to bear the burden
of the heavy choking heat.
The Puerto Ricans are among those who cannot.
They can go nowhere.
They linger on the corners.
They drink.
They turn up the volume of their TV's.

These Puerto Rican children have turned
the Parish House outside water tap on.
I watch them from my window with a vestryman.
No one has given permission.
They splash.
They throw the water into the humid air.
They laugh.
The temperature is close to 100 degrees.
The water lies upon the church yard in puddles.

My vestryman asks me if the church is properly
insured in case of accident.
For of such, Lord, is the Kingdom of God.

These boys have come to the church to steal.
I know that. They are Puerto Ricans.
Little boys. One can smell them across the room.
Sitting in the chairs before me they tell lies
they smile broadly, they squirm, they stare.
One cannot help but like them. I give them candy
and send them along. Lighten their darkness, Lord.

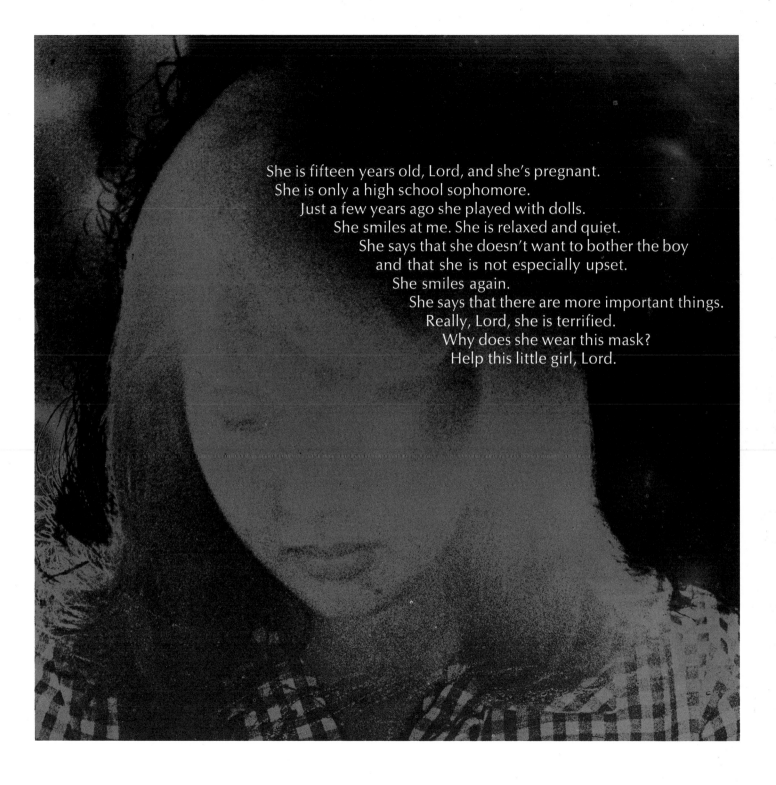

She is fifteen years old, Lord, and she's pregnant.
She is only a high school sophomore.
Just a few years ago she played with dolls.
She smiles at me. She is relaxed and quiet.
She says that she doesn't want to bother the boy
and that she is not especially upset.
She smiles again.
She says that there are more important things.
Really, Lord, she is terrified.
Why does she wear this mask?
Help this little girl, Lord.

This man found his daughter on the living
room couch. Very heavy petting. She is
a high school girl. With the lights on full
he humiliated her in her undress and
cursed her. In my office now he tells me
his daughter hates him and that the very
structure of his family has been badly shaken.
He asks me what to do.
What should he do, Lord?
Let him see how much he himself is
involved here. Let him see that
he must learn to forgive himself and
by this forgiveness to forgive others.

It's up in the North Country, Lord.
County jail.
The guard takes me into a
room filled with old legal
books and high wooden
chairs where I wait for
the boy. It is mid February.
Upstate wintry bleakness.
There is snow and cold.
The boy is out of my
parish. He has been on
a farm since July.
Christmas time he took
the farmer's car without
permission to drive home
to see his family. He
was lonely. He wanted to
be assured of their
love for him. Several hours
later the state police
stopped him with drawn
pistols. The boy is sixteen. He
has no beard. He has been
in jail for two months
awaiting trial. His fellow
inmates are homosexuals
alcoholic derelicts
thieves. The boy looks
bewildered. No money.
No lawyer. No word from
his family. Tomorrow
he tells me, it will be
his turn to clean the
latrines.

It is the Sunday school.
Teen-agers.
Sitting before me
in their chairs.
Glassy-eyed.
I am trying to
teach them, Lord,
but I know they are bored.
Indifferent. They do
not ask the questions
the Church has always
answered.
Why are they here, Lord?
Why this failure?

This teen-age boy standing
first on one foot and then
on the other—twisting his
body about in embarrassment—
is home today from the
hospital. He was unconscious,
Lord, for almost a full day
after swallowing almost
100 aspirin, and next year
he will be in the eleventh grade.
His mother tells him to sit
down. The boy will not look
at us, and in his face so
young and fresh there is
a depression deep and sad.
The mother talks to me
about the church. The boy
sits on the couch wondering
if anyone has heard his
alarm in the night. Let him
know that you have, Lord.

He is twelve.
He is a Negro.
Two months he has
been in the church
choir Tuesday afternoons
Thursday evenings
Sunday mornings. His
mother has said she
thought it good for
the boy. Perhaps he
would learn to sing.
Then, Lord, the boy
does not come to the
choir. The weeks go
by. I go again to see
his mother.
"He doesn't have it"
she says. "He could
never make it in a white
church."

It is a college forum.
The subject is Vietnam.
The students have begun to
question one of the speakers.
I have arrived late and I
am standing in the back of
the great room. There are no
seats. There are many people
standing as I am. The students
now are attacking one of the
speakers with hostility and
rudeness. How, Lord, can they
be so virulent when they are
so young? Is this the fruit
of the Great Society? Affluence?
Have we done this to them?
Have we stirred these deep
wells of hate and anger?

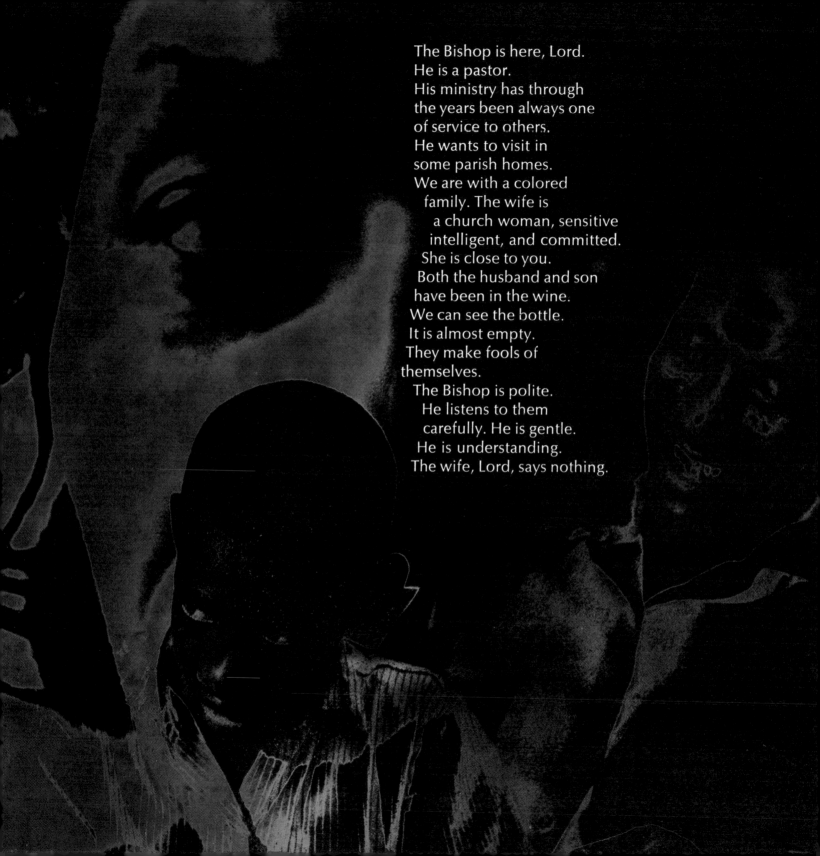

The Bishop is here, Lord.
He is a pastor.
His ministry has through
the years been always one
of service to others.
He wants to visit in
some parish homes.
We are with a colored
   family. The wife is
    a church woman, sensitive
     intelligent, and committed.
    She is close to you.
   Both the husband and son
  have been in the wine.
We can see the bottle.
It is almost empty.
They make fools of
themselves.
   The Bishop is polite.
    He listens to them
     carefully. He is gentle.
    He is understanding.
   The wife, Lord, says nothing.

The telephone rang early
in the morning, Lord.
She said her husband was
beating her. She asked
me please to come. Now she is
sitting in the shadows
where I cannot see her. The
scent of cheap wine
floats across the room. Her six-
year-old boy sleeps
in her lap. She is drunk.
No one has beaten her.
It is the dead of night, Lord.
I am very tired.
Bless this woman.

It was only a weekend, she said.
Just two nights.
They met in Chicago.
He was on business.
She lied to get away from
her home and family.
Her husband doesn't know
doesn't suspect, and never
will know. She is young, Lord,
and sexually attractive and
seemingly unconcerned.
She says that her husband
bores her. He is colorless.
She cannot stay with him
any longer. She says that
her experience in Chicago with
her lover was a crescendo of
intense physical pleasure
beyond anything she had
ever known. What about
your children? I ask. She
glances at her watch. There
is a pause. The question, Lord, is
upon us, the weekend
in Chicago notwithstanding.

Inability to communicate
despite group therapy
the psychiatrist
trips to Europe
and the best social circles
has broken this marriage.
Now voices are raised
no longer. Gone are the
recriminations. There are
no doors to slam. All
talk is done.
Now there are only the
wounds and cynicism of
putting asunder of that
which you, Lord, put
together.

It has been twenty-five years since
they were married.
Nothing so uncommon about
that. Usually an
occasion for a party
with greeting cards
and gifts and
things like that.
They have asked to repeat
their marriage vows.
It is in the evening.
We are alone in the church.
The church is dark and silent
and deep.
To love, honor, and cherish.
In sickness and in health.
This time they understand.
They have known the better
and withstood the worse.
Their marriage is of you, Lord.
They are man and wife.

She has come to see me
in my office and she
believes that she has made
a mistake in her marriage.
She tells me that there
is no doubt in her mind
that she has married the
wrong man. He has never
made any attempt to
understand her or to
cherish her. She is alone.
She wants to separate.
This woman, Lord, is almost
seventy years old. She and her
husband will soon be married
fifty years. Jubilee.
Grandmother figure.
Rocking chair and knitting.
Why now, Lord?
Why after a lifetime?

I am kneeling at my prie-dieu, Lord.
I am reading the Morning Office.
Domine, quis habitabit?
Outside it has begun to rain.
I hear the sound of dripping
water and know that the
church roof is leaking once
again. The budgeted money
for property repairs has
been already spent. There
will be worry and concern
with the vestry. Perhaps
trouble. There is no money.
Roofs and Psalms.
Budgets and Canticles.
Lord, who shall dwell
in your tabernacle?
Or who shall rest upon
your holy hill?

There is a quiet here, Lord,
and it almost seems as if
time had stopped and the
aching pressures of this
day gently lifted.
I am sitting in the pew
listening and resting. I can hear you.
There is much about this, Lord,
that I do not understand, but I do
not try to understand sitting
here in the pew. Here I find strength.
I thank you for that.

He is kneeling here beside me.
Together we eat and drink.
He dislikes me.
    I know that.
I can smell it in him.
    I dislike him.
Bread and wine make no difference.
    Body and blood.
        We go on as before, disliking.
It is our blindness, Lord.
    It is our anguish.

The Bishops are about to begin
their procession down the
Cathedral nave, Lord.
The great organ splits the
air with mighty splendor.
The Bishops' mitres radiate
their ecclesiastic glory
as acolytes scurry along
behind, holding in their
hands the trains of copes
brocades, beads, and majesty.
    Let the sanctus bells be rung!
    Let there be Te Deum sung!
    Let the thurifers cast up
    clouds of holy incense!
The Bishops lift their
ringed fingers heavenward
to bestow upon us manifold
apostolic blessings in the
plenitude of their grace
munificent anachronistic.

It is early, Lord.
So early that the
sun has yet to rise
and one can still
faintly see the stars
of the night, and the
church lies in the
penumbral shadows
and vague light
of the new day.
My eyes and mind
are fresh from
sleep when I see her
kneeling in the
pew. Quietly, Lord.
So quietly. She is
deeply engaged with you,
Lord, and does not
know I am here too
watching her. What
is it, I wonder, that
brings her to her
knees in the church
before the coming
of the morning sun.
I leave her, Lord, to
be alone with you.

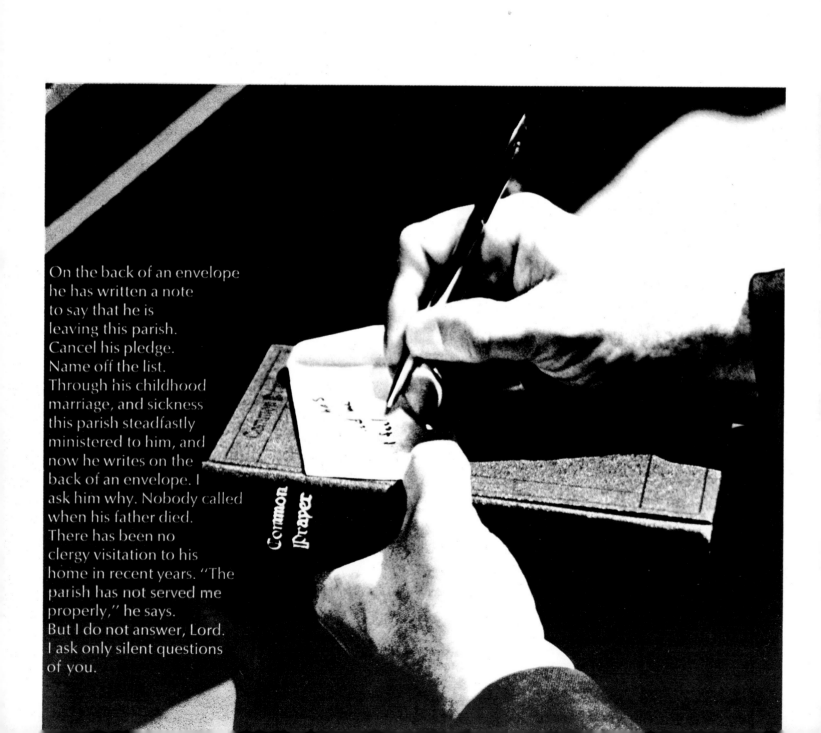

On the back of an envelope
he has written a note
to say that he is
leaving this parish.
Cancel his pledge.
Name off the list.
Through his childhood
marriage, and sickness
this parish steadfastly
ministered to him, and
now he writes on the
back of an envelope. I
ask him why. Nobody called
when his father died.
There has been no
clergy visitation to his
home in recent years. "The
parish has not served me
properly," he says.
But I do not answer, Lord.
I ask only silent questions
of you.

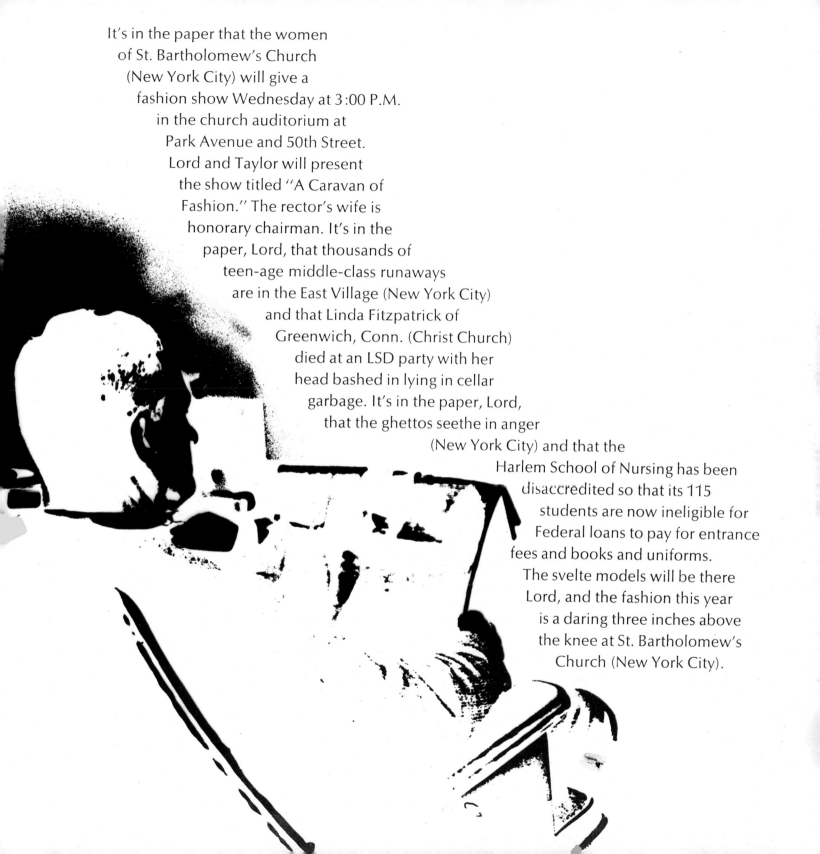

It's in the paper that the women
of St. Bartholomew's Church
(New York City) will give a
fashion show Wednesday at 3:00 P.M.
in the church auditorium at
Park Avenue and 50th Street.
Lord and Taylor will present
the show titled "A Caravan of
Fashion." The rector's wife is
honorary chairman. It's in the
paper, Lord, that thousands of
teen-age middle-class runaways
are in the East Village (New York City)
and that Linda Fitzpatrick of
Greenwich, Conn. (Christ Church)
died at an LSD party with her
head bashed in lying in cellar
garbage. It's in the paper, Lord,
that the ghettos seethe in anger
(New York City) and that the
Harlem School of Nursing has been
disaccredited so that its 115
students are now ineligible for
Federal loans to pay for entrance
fees and books and uniforms.
The svelte models will be there
Lord, and the fashion this year
is a daring three inches above
the knee at St. Bartholomew's
Church (New York City).

Tonight there has been
so much work
so much preparation
and so little response.
It makes me think, Lord,
that there are times
when your church is a
voice speaking in
empty rooms, damp and
stale, to a handful
of embarrassed people
making excuses.

It is the summer congregation, Lord.
The doors of the church lie open.
Outside there is the sun and the cicada's
whirring sound.
Inside there are interminable rows of pews
vacant and musty.
I am a visitor. I do not see you here.
One can see the scattered aged few fanning
themselves with bulletins.
The sermon is about to begin. The supply
sexton yawns. The organist slides
off his bench.
The sermon has to do with Benedict of Nursia
(whose festal day will soon take place)
and in the city a
ten-year-old colored looter lies shot dead
in the street next to a column of tanks
moving by.

Such a small group, Lord.
Only seven or eight
meeting together.
Statistic of failure.
No money, no power.
No influence, no prestige.
Yet we know one another
so well, Lord,
that there is, in this
knowledge, acceptance
and love.
Wounds are healed and masks
removed, and your presence,
Lord, is here upon us.

The light of the setting sun
through the stained glass
is, of course, nothing more
than an aesthetic experience
or perhaps a proper subject for
architects, interior decorators
and the like.
Any fool knows that.
Multicolors flashing
silently across the walls
and onto the floors
beneath—what does it mean?
Very little, replies the world.
Yet it makes me talk in whispers,
Lord. It makes me think of you.

It's the Women's Group, Lord.
Mrs. Gray is annoyed because no
altar flowers were sent to her
in the hospital.
Mrs. Green would prefer to have the
girl choir back in its old position.
Mrs. White is responsible for the
bake sale scheduled for next month.
Mrs. Brown has lost the minutes of last
month's meeting.
Do they know, Lord,
that the gates of hell
cannot prevail
against the Church?

He is the sexton, Lord.
He has been here many
years. I see him sitting
on the stool of the
parish kitchen smoking
Camels, staring into
space, waiting for
someone to talk to.
"He's a good mixer"
people say, and they are
quite right. He is slow
and he does his work
improperly and
halfheartedly, and
sometimes he does not do
what he is asked. "Good old
Casey," people say, and thus
his sins are forgiven, and
I know, Lord, that to fire
the sexton will shake the
foundations of this
congregation and that is
something which racism or
war or poverty has never
been able to do.
One mustn't fire sextons,
Lord, unnecessarily.

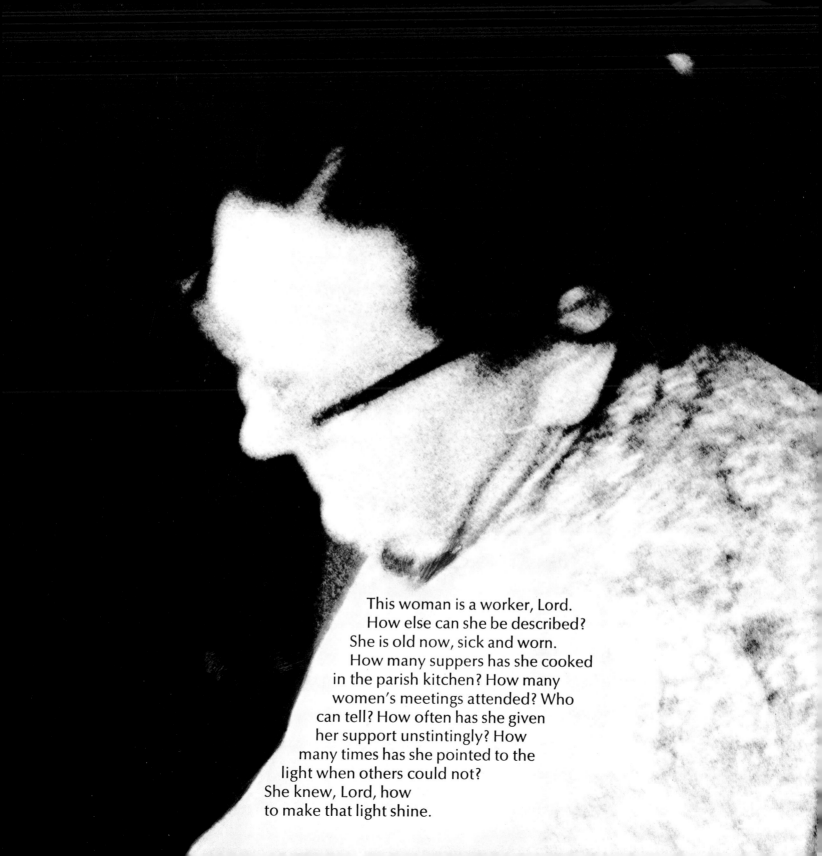

This woman is a worker, Lord.
How else can she be described?
She is old now, sick and worn.
How many suppers has she cooked
in the parish kitchen? How many
women's meetings attended? Who
can tell? How often has she given
her support unstintingly? How
many times has she pointed to the
light when others could not?
She knew, Lord, how
to make that light shine.

He never had much money, Lord.
That is why he is in this home
with these other people aged
and sick on welfare.
In the air one can feel the weight
of suffering and poverty
hanging heavily and oppressively.
He gives me money for the church.
It is in a neat pile of envelopes.
This is where he wants to spend
his money, he argues.

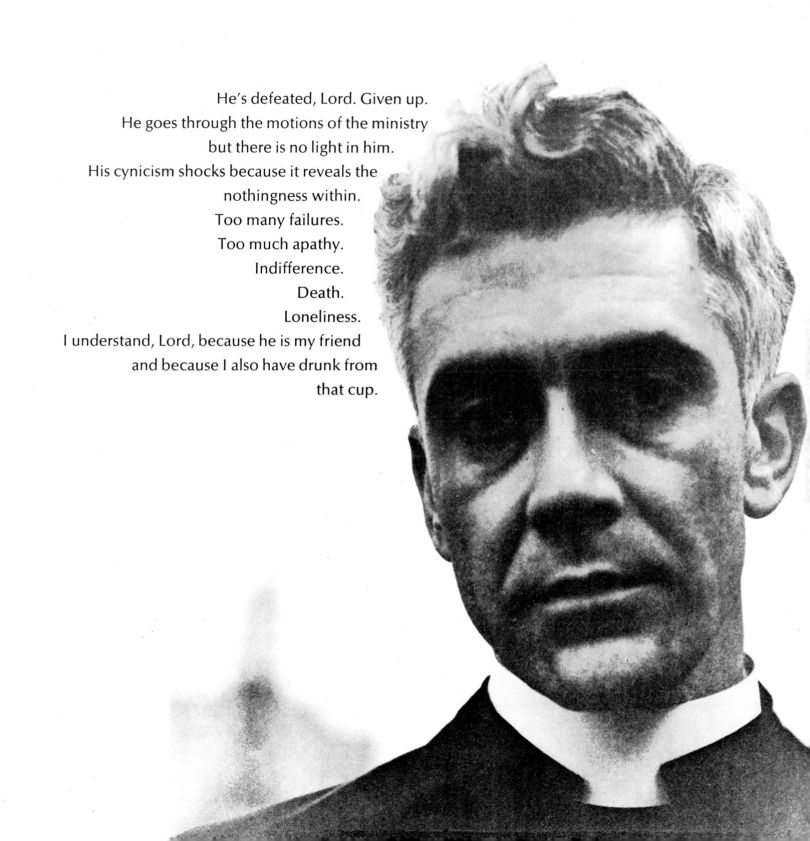

He's defeated, Lord. Given up.
He goes through the motions of the ministry
but there is no light in him.
His cynicism shocks because it reveals the
nothingness within.
Too many failures.
Too much apathy.
Indifference.
Death.
Loneliness.
I understand, Lord, because he is my friend
and because I also have drunk from
that cup.

The study group is in session
once again, Lord, and
tonight I mixed some
Shakespeare with St. Paul.
Contrast. Paul and Hamlet.
It was the passage from
Hamlet when Hamlet says that
the world seems to him
weary, stale, flat and
unprofitable, like an
unweeded garden gone
to seed. One of the women
in the group begins to
cry silently, imperceptibly
for a quick moment. She is
a thirty-five-year-old secretary in
a local insurance office.
She has never married. She
lives alone. Afterwards
when I speak to her she
looks at the floor, Lord, to say
that she always has been
a rather emotional person.

It's just a small group of
old ladies, Lord.
Mostly widows, grandmothers
and the like.
They have been a part of
this parish for many
years. First Monday.
For most of them each month
this is the day they
carefully save.
It is their group and they
have made it.
Tea, dessert, talk, laughter
visiting, gossip.
I know they seldom talk of
you, Lord, but I also
know that
this group
is of you.

Sitting on the bed, Lord,
at night, I look back
across the long hours of
this day and feel now a
sense of weariness. A sense
of nothingness. There has
been this day the minutiae
of busyness. There has been
an endless and exhausting
running and running in the
petty little circles of
church work
and tonight I feel the
fatigue and flat nothingness.
Why? Why?
Where is the meaning?
What the significance?
Take my fatigue, Lord.
Take my nothingness.
Let it become in you
a source
of new life.

It is the Ministerial Association, Lord.
Tea and cookies. Shall we unite
in prayer? Release time. Union
services.
Frayed cuffs.
Camaraderie.
Isolation.
Ideology.
Indebtedness.
We grasp one another's
hands in strength
and in weakness
standing up
for Jesus
once
a month.

This woman's son has
been missing for six months.
Fresh out of the Army, Lord,
he abruptly quit his job
left no forwarding address
and then was swallowed
up, mysteriously gone.
The woman will not go
to the police. Bad
publicity for the family.
She will not hire a private
detective. Much too expensive.
She asks me to say a prayer.

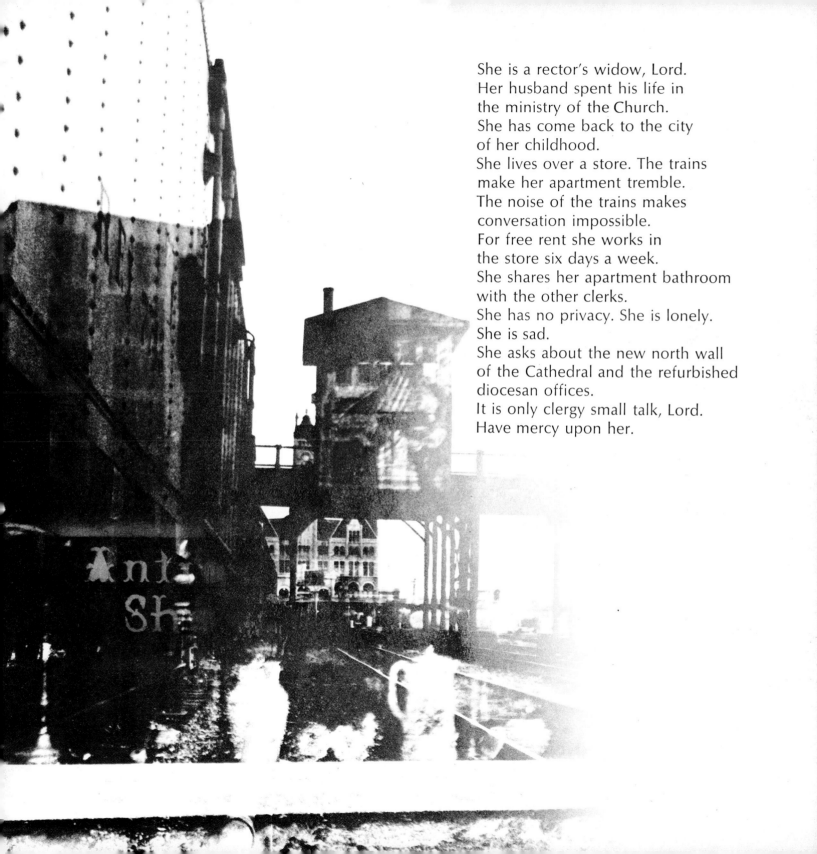

She is a rector's widow, Lord.
Her husband spent his life in
the ministry of the Church.
She has come back to the city
of her childhood.
She lives over a store. The trains
make her apartment tremble.
The noise of the trains makes
conversation impossible.
For free rent she works in
the store six days a week.
She shares her apartment bathroom
with the other clerks.
She has no privacy. She is lonely.
She is sad.
She asks about the new north wall
of the Cathedral and the refurbished
diocesan offices.
It is only clergy small talk, Lord.
Have mercy upon her.

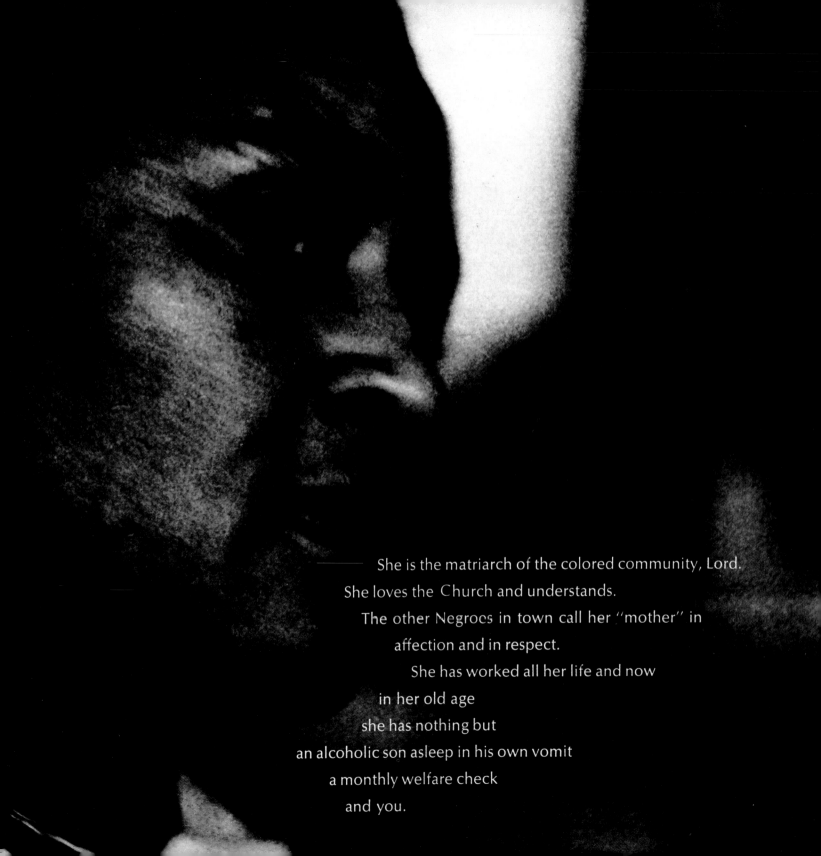

She is the matriarch of the colored community, Lord.
She loves the Church and understands.
The other Negroes in town call her "mother" in
affection and in respect.
She has worked all her life and now
in her old age
she has nothing but
an alcoholic son asleep in his own vomit
a monthly welfare check
and you.

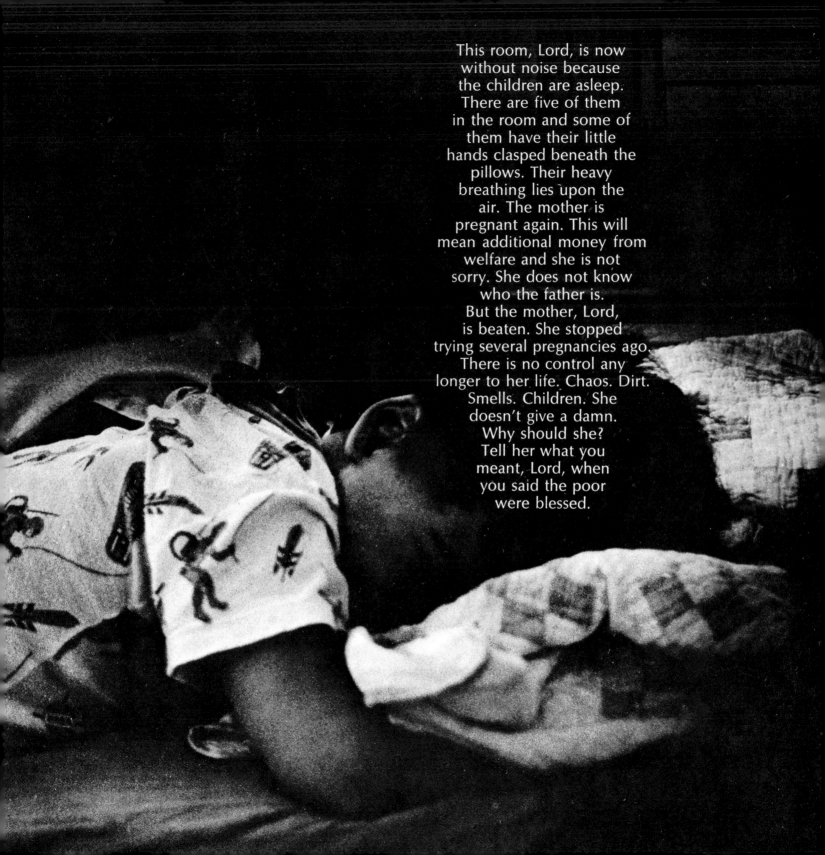

This room, Lord, is now
without noise because
the children are asleep.
There are five of them
in the room and some of
them have their little
hands clasped beneath the
pillows. Their heavy
breathing lies upon the
air. The mother is
pregnant again. This will
mean additional money from
welfare and she is not
sorry. She does not know
who the father is.
But the mother, Lord,
is beaten. She stopped
trying several pregnancies ago.
There is no control any
longer to her life. Chaos. Dirt.
Smells. Children. She
doesn't give a damn.
Why should she?
Tell her what you
meant, Lord, when
you said the poor
were blessed.

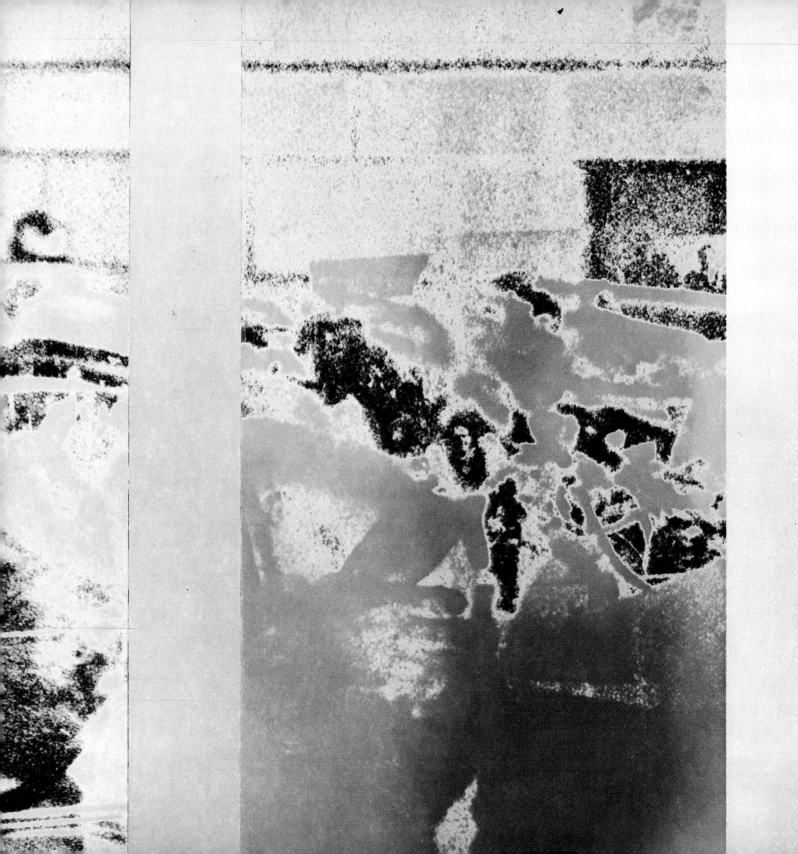

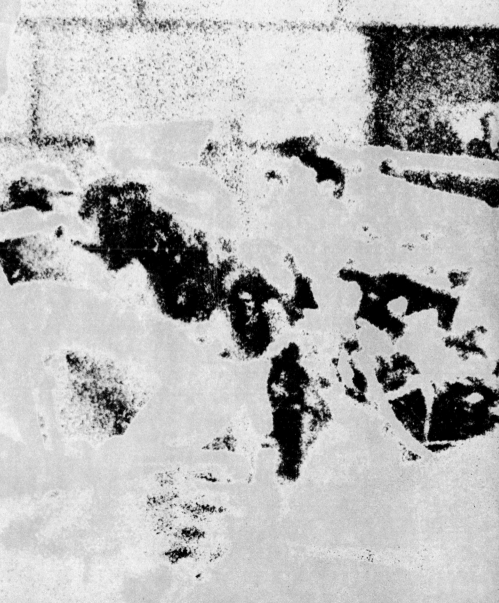

He is the mayor of
metropolis. Clergy
from the suburbs and
the city have come
to hear him. He talks
about the aspirations
of his administration
and of the problems
of the city. Someone
asks what the clergy
might do for the city.
He gropes for an answer,
Lord. He blinks at us.
He suggests that we
might like to give
a talk or two to the
Senior Citizens.

He is the retreat leader, Lord, and I
am listening to him. There is the rule of
silence and in this silence one can
hear anew. He is an old priest at the
end of his life and ministry. Sitting
there in his chair he seems like dayspring
from on high and ancient of days. I listen.
In him there is holiness and wisdom. In him there
is renewal. We sit at his feet. We drink him in.
In him, we can see you.

Her husband, Lord, is
in Vietnam. Green Beret.
Her father was killed in
World War II. Purple Heart.
She is a schoolteacher.
B.A. and M.A.
She has come to teach
third graders.
She is colored.
She needs an apartment.
She wants a proper place
to live.
Shrinking population.
Economic depression.
For Lease.
Still there is nothing.
"After all," one landlord
says to me, "I've got to
protect my investment."

He is Jewish, Lord.
He is talking to me
about anti-Semitism.
His voice trembles
quietly with feeling.
"Christianity is of course
responsible," he says.
"The New Testament is
virulently anti-Semitic."
Very casually he lays
these words before me
and suddenly, Lord, I see
that he is right. Why is
it that I never saw this
obvious fact before
through years of study
years of preaching, years
of ministry? Why have we
so blinded ourselves?
Who can forgive us?

The Rotarians have their badges on, Lord.
Service before self.
R–O–T–A–R–Y—that spells Rotary.
25¢ fine. Ring the bell. Guffaws.
I give my interdenominational blessing.
"Don't ask me to introduce you to any
of these fellows," the president whispers
in my ear. "I only know their first names."
Fellowship of the Holy Ghost, Amen.

She is a Puerto Rican mother, Lord. She and her
whole family are on welfare. I know them. She
has picked a flower from the church yard. "Blanca," she
says with a smile. I tell her to keep the flower.
I ask her to come back again to the church yard.
But she never does.

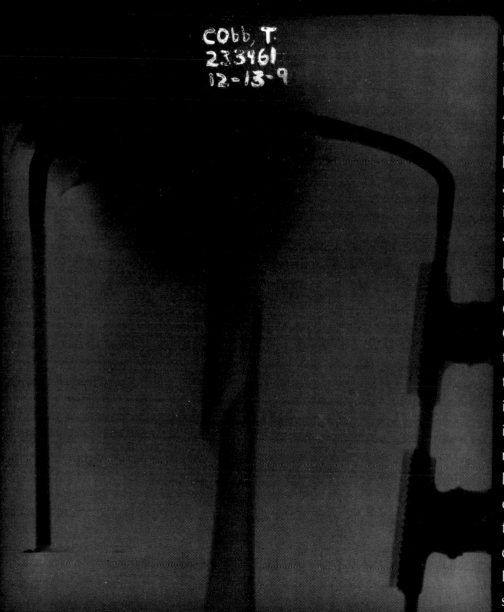

COBB, T.
233461
12-13-9

He's been with the plant
for thirty years. Maintenance
mechanic and troubleshooter.
At his home five weeks ago
in a fall from a ladder
he shattered his hip bone
and leg, and now he lies
in a maze of wires and pulleys
and weights and plaster of
paris. But the bones, Lord,
have not begun to mend.
Calcium deficiency.
Closing his eyes he tells me
that he received word this day
that his salary would be cut off
in three weeks. After thirty years
in three weeks there will be
nothing. He shakes his head
like a big dog and lights another
cigarette. He's never been one
for the Church very much. He
doesn't ask me for any answers.
His room is blue with cigarette
smoke.

He's the publisher of the local paper, Lord.

He is angry. He is shouting.

He thinks it improper that the clergy

should speak out on controversy.

Don't mix religion and politics, he warns.

Not in my paper.

Stay in your pulpit and in your cloister

and keep your Christian Faith

out

of my world.

This woman has tried to kill herself, Lord,
after a bitter argument with her husband.
An overdose of barbituates. She has been in a
coma for two days. They pumped out her stomach.
She is awake now. She looks at me. Her eyes are wild
and puffy. I say nothing. I try to smile. I take
her hand. I can feel her fingers squeezing mine.

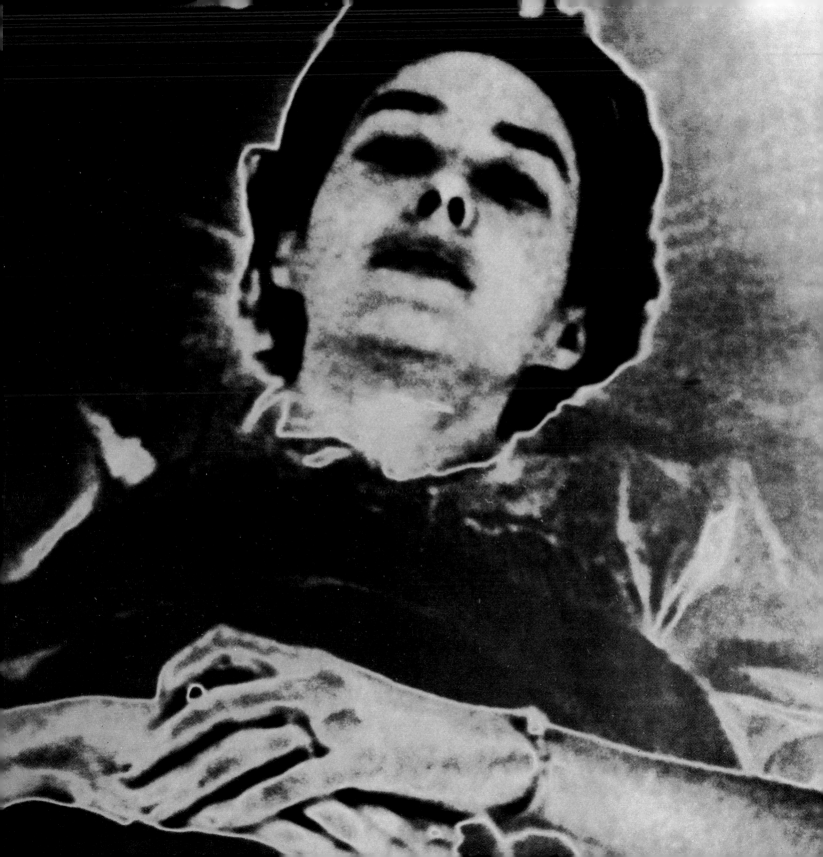

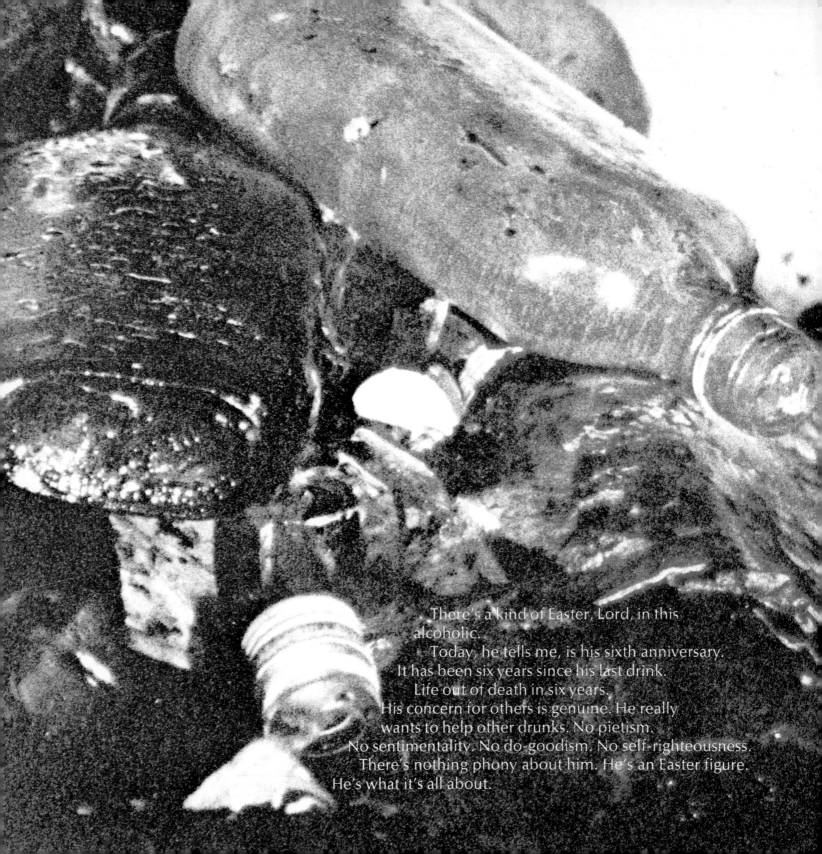

There's a kind of Easter, Lord, in this
alcoholic.
     Today, he tells me, is his sixth anniversary.
It has been six years since his last drink.
     Life out of death in six years.
His concern for others is genuine. He really
     wants to help other drunks. No pietism.
No sentimentality. No do-goodism. No self-righteousness.
     There's nothing phony about him. He's an Easter figure.
He's what it's all about.

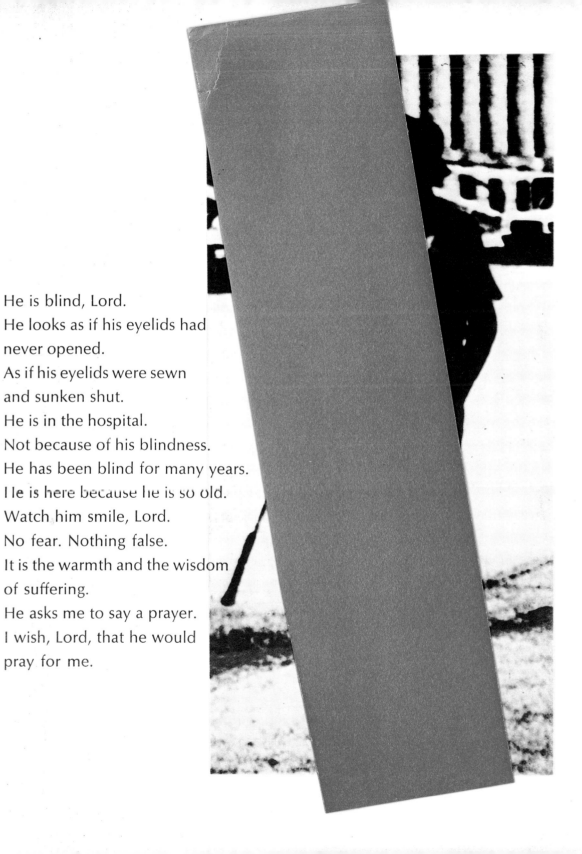

He is blind, Lord.
He looks as if his eyelids had
never opened.
As if his eyelids were sewn
and sunken shut.
He is in the hospital.
Not because of his blindness.
He has been blind for many years.
He is here because he is so old.
Watch him smile, Lord.
No fear. Nothing false.
It is the warmth and the wisdom
of suffering.
He asks me to say a prayer.
I wish, Lord, that he would
pray for me.

It is the laying on of hands, Lord.
She has come because she is ill with cancer
and recently there has been another tumor.
I see her there in the congregation pale and
thin and anxious. She awaits her turn.
Why has she come? She has never come before.
Does she come because nothing else has worked?
Has her family brought her here today? Lord,
I thank you that she is here.
I know why she has come.
She has come to find you.

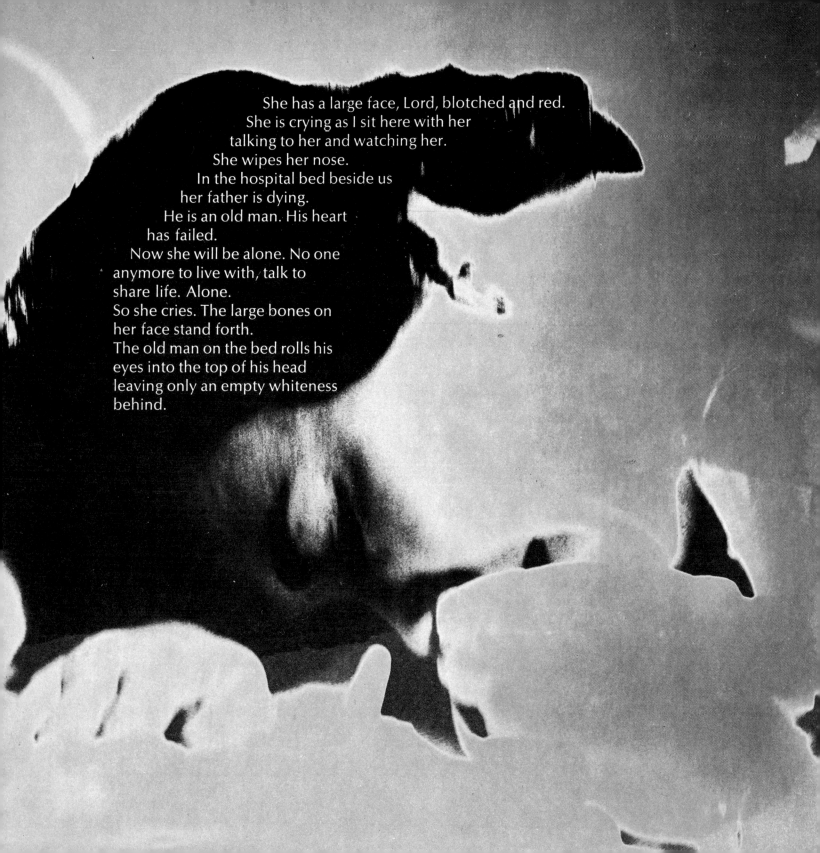

She has a large face, Lord, blotched and red.
She is crying as I sit here with her
talking to her and watching her.
She wipes her nose.
In the hospital bed beside us
her father is dying.
He is an old man. His heart
has failed.
Now she will be alone. No one
anymore to live with, talk to
share life. Alone.
So she cries. The large bones on
her face stand forth.
The old man on the bed rolls his
eyes into the top of his head
leaving only an empty whiteness
behind.

This small girl
in her blue
pajamas sits
up in her bed.
Two days ago
a malignant
tumor on her liver
was surgically
removed. She tells
me of her dog and
her cat and her
grandfather's new
house. There is,
Lord, I know
no answer to
her question.

It is an abandoned church, Lord.
Shabby and worn.
The snow fallen days ago lies
upon its steps undisturbed
dirty and caked.
Inner city casualty.
Church of no congregation.
The weather of many years
has streaked its walls and

laid bare its wood.
Forgotten church. Alone.
Where are those who labored to
build this church? What of
those who worshiped here?
Said prayers here? Sang hymns here?
Does the snow lie upon them too
dirty, caked, and undisturbed?
Let them go from strength to strength.

She's a young woman, Lord.
She's been out of the state
hospital for several years
now. She's been just fine.
Today, though, the torment
has come back. In her eyes,
Lord, I can see pain and
the demon reawakened within.
Her speech and mind, slowed
by drugs, move in thick
torpor. They will say she
is mental again. Backbiters
will backbite. Where can she
shed her blood, Lord?
Where can she let go?
You listen to her, Lord.
Wrap her up in your
wholeness.

This doctor, Lord,
is here although I
know today was to
be his day to rest
and to be alone
with his family
and his friends.
The child is sick.
He has fever.
He has chills.
The doctor has come.
He is not here for
money. There is no
money. He is not here
to strut atop his
pedestal. Pedestals
bore him.
He has come
because he is needed
because he feels
because he has vocation
because you are with him.

It is the doctor, Lord.
Tanned by the Jamaica sun and handsome
he has come into the room.
Retinue of white coats obediently follow
his lead.
I am praying for his patient.
He watches me carefully for a moment
and then walks out, train and all.
Medicine man. Dancing over the sick.
Incantations.
Salvation by stethoscope, fat fee schedules, and
MD license plates.

The old man is dead.
I always liked him.
I thought he was a
good man, Lord. He is
here now beneath the
pall in the church.
The church is empty.
Only the undertaker is
here. He tells me there
is little profit in
welfare burials. The
old man loved the
Church. By the Church
his life was fed. I
know that. Now he is
alone. Now he lies at
the chancel steps.
No one ever paid him
much attention, Lord.
He didn't care. He
found his being
in you.

It happened in the night, Lord.
No one knows at what time.
The baby was found dead in
the crib in the morning.
There are some neighbors here.
I am here too.
In the hall outside there
is no heat. There is the scent
of urine. The plaster is cracked.
The stairs are worn and have
begun to splinter. The family
is so poor, Lord. The mother
sits on the side of the bed
and looks at me. She has many
other children too. They move
quietly about. She asks me to
baptize the baby. I try to explain
but she does not understand. "I
baptize thee in the name of
the Father and the Son and the
Holy Ghost." The baby feels
cold and wizened. The mother
continues to sit on the bed.
The other children stand still.
They move about no longer.

The dead man in his casket has been
magnificently coiffed. Each hair has
been properly situated in its
assigned place. The eyelids are
waxed together. The cheeks are
rouged and the lips have been
made to smile. What is this ghoulish
doll, Lord? Why is it that we are
so terrified of the dust? Why can
we not see that in you there is
no need for this barbarism?

They are bringing him home today, Lord.
There is to be a church funeral.
Resurrection and life.
At the cemetery the soldiers will fire their
rifles and give a flag to his mother.
He will wear his marine uniform with lance
corporal's stripes and posthumous
Purple Heart.
Machine gun wounds in the chest. Nineteen years old.
And now he has come home.
Holy War.
American good against the evil of the world.
Dead boys all dressed up.

The rain has come, Lord.
Driving into the
cemetery there is
mud. Puddles flowing
over their banks
making other puddles
larger yet. Mechanically
the windshield wiper
sweeps the water back. The car
stops.•We are here, Lord.
Man that is born of woman
hath but a short
time to live and
is full of misery.
They do not leave the car,
Lord. They will not
accompany their deceased
to his grave. Dust to
dust. They prefer to
remain in the car.
They want to stay dry.

Last night this man went
through the windshield, Lord.
2:00 A.M. The state police. DOA.
The undertaker has carefully
explained to the family why
it is that the body cannot
be shown. Death on the highway
alone at night. I am speaking to
the family. The children also
are here. I can hear myself
looking, looking for words
that do not come and I ask,
Lord, that you might show us
the Easter to this Good Friday.

Photographs—James R. Finney

Designer—Nancy Bozeman

Type—12 pt. Optima

Typesetter—Dayton Typographic Service

Manufacturer—Parthenon Press

Printing Process   Offset—2 colors Black on Black

Paper—Body - 80# White Mountie Matte

Endsheets - 50# Beckett Black

Binding—Kivar #5 White—Antique grain—Box back case